50 Healthy Recipes for Your Slow Cooker

Simple and Scrumptious Recipes to Make Your Life Simpler and Yummier

Contents

Disclaimer

This book is the property of the author and any reproduction whether mechanical or digital needs to be properly authorized. This includes photocopying, scanning and any other form of print or recording. The author has taken all measures to provide accurate and factual information, however any changes in facts or figures at a later date are unforeseeable and thus subject to change.

This book is solely for educational purposes and should be taken as such. The author cannot be held responsible for any damages incurred due to the misappropriation of any of the contents of this book.

INTRODUCTION

Chicken consumption per capita has been increasing almost every year since the 1960's, or ever since food consumption has been properly monitored. New ingredients may be introduced in the market, fancier restaurants may have popped up at every corner of the street, but humans' cravings for chicken remain the same, if not increased. Chicken can easily be touted as the ultimate favorite when it comes to the preferences of meat lovers. Hence, meal creators too are more focused on making this world favorite all the more delectable, juicier and easier to cook.

People have one common complaint with meals prepared on the slow cooker- all the meals tend to taste the same. It is like saying every pizza tastes the same simply because each one contains dough, cheese and tomato sauce. The fact is, you aren't experimenting enough. This book will definitely bring out the slow cooker meal creator in you.

This book is a collection of recipes that have utilized the convenience and flavor enhancing methodology of the slow cooker to create meals that are small meaty wonders of their own. When paired with the slow cooker, chicken recipes become relentlessly appetizing. So it is just about time you took the slow cooker out of the garage and allowed it to become the star appliance in your kitchen by creating wonders day after day.

Introduction to Slow Cookers

Slow Cooker or Crock-Pot as it is generally known is a lidded oval or round cooking pot which is made from porcelain or glazed ceramic with a metal housing containing the electric heat element. The lid is most commonly glass.

All you need to do is assemble the ingredients in the morning and switch the cooker on. You can easily go about doing your days work, and by the time you are back, your meal would be hot and ready to be devoured. Slow cookers usually come with two or more temperature settings and use very little energy, which means it wouldn't weigh much on your electricity bill or heat up the kitchen the way your oven does, thus limiting any fire hazards.

Slow cookers come in various shapes and sizes ranging from tiny 1-cup slow cookers to larger sizes that can easily cook meals for a family of 4 or even 6. Slow cookers have evolved from simple settings of low and high temperature. Today they come with sophisticated controls that allow you to delay cooking time, keep the food warm once cooked and different programmed settings for cooking specific dishes.

Why Cook in a Slow Cooker?

Slow cooker sales are booming all over. More and more people are opting for these small yet powerful devices to bring convenience and healthy eating back in their life. Nothing is better than coming home to a ready to eat steaming casserole or stew sitting on the kitchen counter.

Meals prepared in the slow cooker are easy on the pocket, easier to cook and the appliance easiest to use. That's a lot of easy in your lifestyle that you can almost get addicted to. But that's not the end. Cooking in the slow cooker has various other benefits also that have been stated below:

1. Tougher cuts of meat become tender more easily in the slow cooker due to condensation. So you can easily purchase cheaper cuts of meat and yet get full flavor and create tastier meals using less expensive cuts.

2. Vegetables absorb relatively more spices and stocks in the slow cooker, giving them fuller flavors.
3. You can easily adjust the temperature and time on the slow cooker so you don't have to continuously monitor the cooking.
4. Slow cookers are known to prepare meals in 8 to 10 hours, which may be true for some specific meals, but slow cookers today can prepare meals much faster.
5. Slow cooker recipes can be created using limited ingredients thus reduce further cost as well as less preparation time and mess.
6. Don't mistake the multi-cookers for slow cookers, the former have heat elements only at the bottom which can easily burn the dishes.

Slow Cooker Cooking Tips

Following are a list of tried and tested cooking tips to cook the juiciest and most flavorful dishes every time:

I. Fill the slow cooker with about ¾ or preferably ½ of ingredient for best results.

II. Spray the crock with good quality non-stick vegetable spray before you pour in the ingredients. It will prevent the food from sticking to the sides and will make cleaning the equipment very easy.

III. You don't need to add any liquid to the slow cooker. There is no evaporation and so the dishes are cooked with the juices from the ingredients. You might need to add very little liquid in some recipes, in which case it will be mentioned.

IV. Every time you take the lid off, the cooking time increases by a good 15 to 20 minutes. So no peeking!

V. You can adjust the seasonings at the end of the cooking. It is quite difficult to assess the flavors and seasoning beforehand. The flavors of herbs become milder during cooking too, so you may need more based on your own liking, so make sure you taste before you serve.

VI. Slow cooking takes longer at higher altitudes, so add an extra half an hour of cooking time to each hour of every recipe if you are cooking in higher altitudes.

VII. You don't need to add oil to recipes prepared in the slow cooker and you don't need any fat on the meats either. Any fat that's on the meat will not drain away as is the case with normal cooking methods, so make sure you trim most of it away before cooking.

VIII. The liquid will neither reduce nor thicken as it cooks. If you would like the broth to be thicker, add a little cornflour at the end (around a teaspoon or two) or roll the meat with seasoned flour before adding it to the slow cooker.

IX.   Some recipes require browning of some of the ingredients before adding them to the slow cooker. Browning them on the pan will save you a lot of time. However, you can cook them in the slow cooker before adding the rest of the ingredients.

X.   Always soak dried beans before cooking. It will reduce the cooking time to 8 hours rather than the standard 18 hours it takes to cook dried beans directly.

XI.   Slow cooker recipes don't stand well to room temperature, so make sure you refrigerate them immediately once they are cooled off. Don't keep a slow cooker recipe at room temperature for more than two hours.

The Cooking Duration Difference Between Standard Cooking and Slow Cooker Cooking

It takes longer for a dish to cook in a slow cooker. But what's the difference like really? Following chart shows the usual time difference.

If A Dish Usually Takes	On High Speed Cook It For	On Low Speed Cook It For
15-30 minutes	1-2 hours	4-6 hours
30 minutes – 1 hour	2-3 hours	5-7 hours
1-2 hours	3-4 hours	6-8 hours
2-4 hours	4-6 hours	8-12 hours

Measurement Guidelines

It is important that you keep the size of the slow cooker in mind when cooking recipes. If you have to buy just one slow cooker then make sure you purchase a larger model, if you are cooking for more than one person. Preferably purchase at least a 6-quarts model. Most recipes suitable for smaller models can easily be made in the larger pot; however, it is not possible the other way round. Following chart shows measurement equivalents to help you properly measure ingredients:

1 tablespoon (tbsp)	3 teaspoons (tsp)
1 tbsp	1/16 cup
2 tbsp	1/8 cup
2 tbsp + 2 tsp	1/6 cup
5 tbsp + 1tsp	1/3 cup
8 tbsp	½ cup
16 tbsp	1 cup
1 quart	4 cups

Now that you have the basics of cooking in a slow cooker covered, it is time to jump right in and get cooking!

RECIPES FOR EVERY TASTE AND LIFESTYLE

Lunch Recipes

1. Creamy Chicken with Biscuits

Serves: 6

Slow Cooker Size: 4- to 6- quart

Preparation time: 15 Minutes

Cooking Time: 6 Hours

Ingredients:

   i.   8 boneless, skinless chicken thighs
   ii.   ½ cup chicken broth (preferably low sodium)
   iii.   4 large carrots, cut in 1-inch lengths
   iv.   1 small onion, chopped
   v.   2 stalks celery, thinly sliced
   vi.   ½ tsp poultry seasoning
   vii.   ¼ cup all purpose flour
   viii.   1 cup frozen peas

ix.   ½ cup dry white wine

x.   ½ cup heavy cream

xi.   Salt and black pepper to taste

xii.   6 salty biscuits or crackers of your choice

Method:

1. Add flour, carrots, onion to the slow cooker. Place the chicken on top of these ingredients.

2. Season with salt, pepper and poultry seasoning. In the end, add the broth and wine.

3. Cover and cook on high for about 3 hours or on low for about 5 to 6 hours

4. Add the cream, peas and a little more salt if required ten minutes before serving.

5. Serve with biscuits on the bottom and top of the creamy chicken serving.

2. Chicken Tikka Masala

Serves: 4

Slow Cooker Size: 4- to 6- quart

Preparation time: 10 Minutes

Cooking Time: 8 Hours

Ingredient List:

i. 8 boneless, skinless chicken thighs

ii. 1 can of crushed tomatoes, 15 ounce

iii. 2 cloves of garlic, chopped

iv. 1 medium sized onion, chopped

v. 2 tbsp tomato paste

vi. Salt and black pepper to taste

vii. 2 tsp Indian spice blend

viii. ½ cup heavy cream

ix. 1 cup long grain white rice

x. 1 tbsp fresh lemon juice

xi. ¼ cup cilantro leaves, fresh

xii. ½ cucumber, thinly sliced

Method:

1. Add onion, tomatoes, tomato paste, garlic, Indian spice, ¼ tsp pepper, ¾ tsp salt and in the end the chicken to the slow cooker. Cover and cook for 7 to 8 hours on Low or 3 to 4 hours on high speed.
2. Add the cilantro, cucumber, lemon juice and the remaining salt and pepper in a bowl and toss.
3. Cook the rice according to package instructions 20 minutes before the cooking time is up.
4. Once the chicken is cooked, add the cream mix well and serve it with rice and cucumber salad.

3. Chicken and Pasta Soup

Serves: 6

Slow Cooker Size: 5- to 6- quart

Preparation time: 5 Minutes

Cooking Time: 5 Hours

Ingredients:

i. 6 boneless chicken thighs

ii. ½ cup pasta, opt for alphabet or stellette

iii. 4 carrots, cut in 1 inch long pieces

iv. 1 medium onion, halved

v. 2 bay leaves

vi. 2 garlic cloves, smashed

vii. ¼ cup chopped parsley

viii. 4 stalks of celery, cut in ½ inch pieces

ix. Salt and pepper for seasoning

x. Crackers for serving (optional)

Method:

1. Add carrots, celery, garlic, onion, 6 cups of water, salt and pepper and chicken to the Crockpot.

2. Cover the pot and cook for 4 to 5 hours on high or 7 to 8 hours on low heat.
3. Transfer the chicken to a bowl 20 minutes before serving and remove the bay leaves and the onion.
4. Shred the chicken.
5. Meanwhile, add the pasta to the slow cooker and cook for about 18 minutes.
6. Once the pasta is ready, add the shredded chicken and parsley in the soup.
7. Serve with crackers (optional).

4. Chicken and Bacon Recipe

Serves: 6

Slow Cooker Size: 4- to 6- quart

Preparation time: 35 Minutes

Cooking Time: 7 Hours

Ingredients:

i. 4 pound chicken, cut up
ii. ½ pound sliced bacon, diced
iii. ½ pound white mushrooms
iv. ½ cup dry white wine
v. 6 garlic cloves
vi. 1 cup frozen small white onions (thaw before use)
vii. 3 sprigs fresh rosemary
viii. Salt to taste
ix. 2 tbsp cornstarch
x. ¼ cup water

Method:

1. Cook the bacon on medium-low heat in a large skillet. Transfer the bacon to the slow cooker.

2. Next cook the chicken on the skillet until brown and transfer it to the cooker too.
3. Pour the wine in the skillet to scrape off bacon and chicken bits and then add the contents to the slow cooker.
4. Add onions, mushrooms, rosemary, salt and garlic to the slow cooker and cook for 3 hours on high speed or 6 hours on low speed.
5. Add the sauce from the cooker to the skillet and the rest of the ingredients to a platter. Cook the sauce along with the cornstarch and water until it thickens, or for about 5 minutes.
6. Pour over the bacon and chicken and serve while hot.

5. White Bean and Fennel Recipe

Serves: 6

Slow Cooker Size: 4- to 6- quart

Preparation time: 15 Minutes

Cooking Time: 8 Hours

Ingredients:

i. 4 boneless chicken thighs
ii. 4 carrots
iii. 8 cups chicken broth (preferably low-sodium)
iv. 2 stalks celery, chopped
v. 1 large onion, chopped
vi. 1 large fennel bulb, chopped
vii. 1 cup dried white beans
viii. 2 dried bay leaves
ix. ½ cup small pasta
x. Salt and pepper for taste
xi. Country bread for serving (optional)

Method:

1. Combine carrots, chicken, broth, celery, onion, fennel, beans, salt and pepper and bay leaves in the slow cooker.
2. Cover and cook for about 4 to 5 hours on high or 7 to 8 hours on low setting.
3. Twenty minutes before serving take out the chicken in a bowl and cook the pasta on high setting.
4. Discard the bay leaves and shred the pasta.
5. Serve the chicken with the pasta soup and bread.

6. Chicken Verde

Serves: 6

Slow Cooker Size: 6- quart

Preparation time: 15 Minutes

Cooking Time: 4 Hours

Ingredients:

i. 6 bone-in chicken breast halves, skinned
ii. 4 jalapeno peppers
iii. 5 poblano chilies
iv. 1 large onion, chopped
v. 5 garlic cloves, minced
vi. 5 ½ cups chopped tomatillos
vii. 1 tbsp sugar
viii. 1 can chopped green chilies, drained
ix. ½ tsp ground cumin
x. 1 tbsp canola oil
xi. Salt and pepper to taste
xii. 1/3 cup sour cream
xiii. ¼ cup chopped cilantro

Method:

1. Broil the jalapeno peppers and poblano chilies in the broiler for ten minutes or until charred, turn occasionally. Peel the peppers once cool and cut in half in length. Discard the membrane and seeds. Finely chop the jalapeno peppers and poblano chilies.

2. Add the tomatillos, jalapeno peppers, poblano chilies, onions, sugar, garlic and green chilies in a large bowl.

3. Sprinkle the chicken with pepper and cumin and cook it on medium-high heat in a large skillet until brown on both sides.

4. Add the chicken in the slow cooker along with the tomatillo mixture. Cook on low heat for about 3 and a half hours.

5. Remove the chicken and pour the sauce in a saucepan and bring to a boil. Reduce the heat and cook uncovered until the liquid is reduced to about 4 cups.

6. Serve the sauce with chicken and garnish with cream and chopped cilantro.

7. Spicy Chicken and Rice

Serves: 6

Slow Cooker Size: 5- quart

Preparation time: 15 Minutes

Cooking Time: 5 Hours

Ingredients:

  i.   6 skinned chicken thighs
 ii.   1 can stewed tomatoes, chopped
iii.   6 skinned chicken drumsticks
 iv.   1/3 cup finely chopped onion
  v.   1 tsp canola oil
 vi.   1/3 cup dry white wine
vii.   ½ tsp salt-free lemon-herb seasoning
viii. ¼ tsp salt
 ix.   ½ tsp dried Italian seasoning
  x.   2 garlic cloves, minced
 xi.   3 cups hot cooked rice
xii.   ¼ tsp crushed red pepper
xiii. ¼ tsp dried tarragon

Method:

1. Trim all the fat from the chicken.
2. Heat a large skillet over medium heat and coat it with the oil.
3. Add chicken to it and cook until browned, turning occasionally, will take around 6 minutes.
4. Add the chicken to the slow cooker.
5. Sautee onion and garlic on the skillet for about two minutes. Add wine and tomatoes next. Remove from heat and add Italian seasoning, lemon-herb seasoning, salt, red pepper and dried tarragon.
6. Add this tomato mixture over the chicken in the slow cooker.
7. Cover and cook for 5 hours on Low setting.
8. Serve with cooked rice.

8. Pulled Chicken Sandwiches

Serves: 8

Slow Cooker Size: 4- quart

Preparation time: 15 Minutes

Cooking Time: 4 Hours

Ingredients:

I. 4 skinless, boneless chicken breasts, halved

II. 3 cups thinly sliced onion

III. 1 cup ketchup

IV. 1 tsp canola oil

V. 2 tbsp cider vinegar

VI. 1 tbsp Dijon mustard

VII. 2 tbsp molasses

VIII. ½ tsp garlic powder

IX. 1 tsp onion powder

X. ½ tsp hot sauce

XI. 1 tsp ground cumin

XII. 8 whole-wheat hamburger buns

Method:

1. Add the onions in the slow cooker.
2. Heat a large skillet and add oil to it. Cook the chicken in the skillet until golden brown on both sides, around 6-7 minutes.
3. Add the chicken over the onions in the slow cooker.
4. Add ketchup with the rest of the ingredients (except the buns) and pour over the chicken.
5. Cook on Low setting for 4 hours.
6. Remove the chicken from the cooker when fully cooked and shred it using two forks.
7. Mix the shredded chicken in the sauce.
8. Toast the buns.
9. Add about ¾ cup of chicken mixture to the bottom bun and then cover with the top bun.

9. Sweet Chicken Thighs

Serves: 6

Slow Cooker Size: 4- quart

Preparation time: 15 Minutes

Cooking Time: 3 Hours

Ingredients:

I.   2 pounds skinless, boneless chicken thighs

II.   Cooking spray

III.   1 cup pineapple juice

IV.   Salt and pepper to taste

V.   2 tbsp light brown sugar

VI.   3 tbsp water

VII.   3 tbsp sliced green onions

VIII. 2 tbsp cornstarch

IX.   2 tbsp lower-sodium soy sauce

X.   1 tbsp olive oil

XI.   3 cups cooked rice

Method:

1. Sprinkle salt and pepper on the chicken.
2. Heat oil in a large skillet and cook chicken on the skillet for about 3 minutes on each side, or until browned.
3. Transfer the chicken to the slow cooker.
4. Add the pineapple juice to the skillet to scrape off chicken scraping from the pan. Remove the skillet from pan and add soy sauce and brown sugar.
5. Pour this mixture over the chicken and cook for about 2 hours and 45 minutes on Low setting.
6. Transfer only the chicken on to a platter and increase the heat to High on the slow cooker.
7. Mix 3 tbsp of water and cornstarch in a bowl and add this to the sauce in the slow cooker. Mix well and cook for about 2-3 minutes, or until the sauce thickens. Be sure to constantly stir while the sauce cooks.
8. Serve with a serving of rice topped with the chicken thighs and sauce. Sprinkle with green onions.

10. Chicken Enchilada

Serves: 8

Slow Cooker Size: 5- quart

Preparation time: 20 Minutes

Cooking Time: 2 Hours

Ingredients:

i.   2 cups rotisserie chicken breast

ii.   1 tsp canola oil

iii. ½ cup chopped seeded chili

iv.   1 can no-salt added diced tomatoes

v.   Cooking spray

vi.   1 cup frozen baby corn

vii. 1 cup chopped onion

viii. 2 garlic cloves, minced

ix.   1 ½ tsp chipotle chili powder

x.   Cilantro sprigs

xi.   2 cups shredded cheddar cheese

xii. 5 corn and flour tortillas

xiii. 1 can tomato sauce with garlic, basil and oregano

xiv. 1 can black beans, rinse and drained

Method:

1. Heat a large skillet over medium heat. Heat oil and add poblano chili, garlic and onion and cook until the vegetables are tender, around 6 minutes.
2. Add tomatoes, tomato sauce and chili powder to the skillet and blend well.
3. Blend the tomato mixture in the blender until almost smooth, blend in two batches to avoid overflow.
4. Coat the slow cooker with cooking spray and add about 3 tbsp of the tomato mixture to it. Combine the rest of the mixture with corn, beans and chicken.
5. Place a tortilla over the sauce in the slow cooker and pour about 1 cup chicken mixture on top. Sprinkle it with 1/3 cup of cheddar cheese and then top it with another tortilla. Repeat with the remaining chicken, cheese and tortillas.
6. Cover and cook on Low for about 2 hours or until the edges are lightly browned.

7. Cut into 8 wedges and garnish with cilantro.

11. Asian Chicken

Serves: 8

Slow Cooker Size: 5- quart

Preparation time: 20 Minutes

Cooking Time: 6 Hours

Ingredients:

i. 2 pounds boneless chicken thighs, cut into 1 ½ inch cubes

ii. ½ cup plain yogurt

iii. 1 can diced tomatoes, drained

iv. 2 tbsp minced ginger

v. 1 onion, coarsely chopped

vi. 2 tsp curry powder

vii. 1 large baking potato, peeled and cubed

viii. ½ tsp ground cumin

ix. 1 tsp ground coriander

x. ½ tsp crushed red pepper

xi. 1 tsp salt

xii. 2 bay leaves

xiii. 1 cinnamon stick

xiv. 4 cups long-grain brown rice

xv.   ¼ cup fresh cilantro

Method:

1. Sautee the chicken on high heat on a large skillet for about 8 minutes, or until lightly browned.
2. Add the chicken to the slow cooker.
3. Cook the onion in the pan for about 3 minutes. Add ginger, curry powder, cumin, coriander, red pepper and garlic to the onions.
4. Add this mixture over the chicken along with potato, cinnamon stick, tomatoes, bay leaves and salt.
5. Cover and cook on Low setting for 6 hours. Remove the cinnamon stick and bay leaves once finished.
6. Mix the yogurt in the chicken.
7. Serve the chicken with rice. Sprinkle cilantro for garnish.

12. Mediterranean Chicken

Serves: 6

Slow Cooker Size: 5- quart

Preparation time: 15 Minutes

Cooking Time: 4 Hours

Ingredients:

i. 12 bone-in chicken thighs, skinned
ii. 1 onion, coarsely chopped
iii. 1 small lemon
iv. 1 can whole plum tomatoes, coarsely chopped
v. 2 tbsp drained capers
vi. 1 tbsp olive oil
vii. 12 pitted kalamata olives, halved
viii. Fresh rosemary and parsley, chopped

Method:

1. Grate, rind and squeeze juice from lemon.
   Place the rind in a bowl, cover and refrigerate.
2. Add onion, lemon, olives, capers, tomatoes in
   the slow cooker.

3. Sprinkle pepper on chicken and cook on the skillet until browned from both sides (as prepared in previous recipes). Add the chicken in the slow cooker and cook on Low setting for 4 hours.
4. Place the chicken thighs on a platter.
5. Add the rinds to the sauce and serve over the chicken. Garnish with parsley and rosemary.

13. Sweet and Sour Chicken

Serves: 6

Slow Cooker Size: 5- 6- quart

Preparation time: 20 Minutes

Cooking Time: 6 Hours

Ingredients:

i. 4 chicken leg quarters

ii. 2 tsp ground cumin

iii. 3 garlic cloves, minced

iv. 1 can diced tomatoes

v. 3 inch fresh ginger, peeled and sliced

vi. 1 tbsp extra-virgin olive oil

vii. Salt and pepper to taste

viii. ½ tsp ground cinnamon

ix. 1 medium onion, cut in small wedges

x. ½ cup raisins

Method:

1. Combine cinnamon, salt, cumin, pepper in a zip-top bag and mix, then chicken and toss to coat.
2. Heat a large skillet and cook until browned on both sides, around 6 minutes.
3. Place garlic, onion and ginger in the slow cooker. Add the chicken, tomatoes with liquid and raisins.
4. Cover and cook for about 6 hours on Low or 3 ½ hours on high.
5. Serve with rice or bread.

14. Chicken and Orange

Serves: 4

Slow Cooker Size: 4- to 6- quart

Preparation time: 15 Minutes

Cooking Time:4 Hours

Ingredients:

i.   4 skinless chicken thighs

ii.   ½ cup orange marmalade

iii. ½ cup orange juice

iv.   1 clove garlic, minced

v.   ¼ cup soy sauce

vi.   Flour for dredging

vii. 2 tbsp ketchup

viii. 2 cups boiled rice

Method:

1. Remove all visible fat from the chicken.
2. Roll the chicken in flour until fully coated.
3. Add the chicken to the slow cooker.
4. Combine all the remaining ingredients in a bowl and pour over the thighs.

5. Cover and cook for 4 hours on Low setting.
6. Remove the chicken and sauce and serve with boiled rice.

15. Chicken and Beans

Serves: 4

Slow Cooker Size: 5- to 6- quart

Preparation time: 15 Minutes

Cooking Time: 8 Hours

Ingredients:

i.   8 boneless, skinless chicken thighs

ii.   2 tbsp chopped canned chipotle chilies

iii.   1 jar mild salsa

iv.   1 cup dried pinto beans, rinsed

v.   Salt and pepper to taste

vi.   2 tbsp all-purpose flour

vii.   1 medium red onion, chopped

viii.   ¼ cup sour cream

ix.   ¼ cup chopped fresh cilantro

x.   1 red bell pepper, chopped with seeds removed

Method:

1. Add beans, chilies, flour, salsa and 1 cup water in the slow cooker and mix well.
2. Season the chicken with salt and pepper and add that to the salsa mixture.
3. Cover and cook for 8 hours.
4. Remove the chicken and shred in large pieces. Add the chicken pieces to the stew and serve topped with cilantro and sour cream.

Dinner Recipes

16. Chicken with Potato and Carrots

Serves: 6

Slow Cooker Size: 6- quart

Preparation time: 15 Minutes

Cooking Time: 3 ½ Hours

Ingredients:

i. 6 chicken thighs, skinned
ii. 1 onion, vertically sliced
iii. 2 cups baby carrots
iv. ½ cup chicken broth
v. 6 small red potatoes, cut in thin slices
vi. 1 tbsp chopped fresh thyme
vii. 1 tsp paprika
viii. 1 tsp olive oil
ix. Salt and pepper to taste
x. 1 tsp minced garlic
xi. ½ cup dry white wine

Method:

1. Add the potatoes, carrots and onions in the slow cooker.

2. In a large bowl combine the chicken broth, salt and pepper, wine, thyme and garlic and mix well. Pour this mixture over the vegetables in the slow cooker.

3. Combine paprika with a little salt and pepper and rub over the chicken. Cook the chicken on a large skillet until browned on both sides, about 6 minutes.

4. Place the chicken on top of the vegetables. Cover and cook on Low setting for about 3 ½ hours or until chicken is fully cooked.

17. Curried Chicken

Serves: 6

Slow Cooker Size: 4- to 6- quart

Preparation time: 15 Minutes

Cooking Time: 8 Hours

Ingredients:

i.   10 boneless, skinless chicken thighs

ii.   1/3 cup tomato paste

iii.   1 tbsp grated fresh ginger

iv.   1 ½ cup white rice, cooked

v.   2 scallions thinly sliced

vi.   1 tsp ground cumin

vii.   4 cloves garlic, chopped

viii.   1 tbsp fresh ginger

ix.   2 tbsp curry powder

x.   1 onion, chopped

xi.   Salt and pepper to taste

xii.   ½ cup Greek yogurt

Method:

1. Whisk ginger, ¾ cup water, tomato paste, garlic, cumin and curry powder together. Add onion and blend well. Add this paste to the slow cooker.
2. Season the chicken with salt and pepper and place on the paste in the slow cooker.
3. Cover and cook on Low setting for 8 hours.
4. Add yogurt and a little more salt, if desired right before serving.
5. Serve with rice and top with sliced scallions.

18. Soy Braised Chicken

Serves: 4

Slow Cooker Size: 5- to 6- quart

Preparation time: 10 Minutes

Cooking Time: 8 Hours

Ingredients:

i.   8 skinless chicken thighs

ii.   2 medium sized onions, sliced

iii.   1/3 cup apple cider vinegar

iv.   1 tbsp brown sugar

v.   Salt and pepper to taste

vi.   1 tsp paprika

vii.   1 cup white rice, cooked

viii.   4 garlic cloves, smashed

ix.   1/3 cup soy sauce

x.   1 large head bok choy (Chinese cabbage), cut in small strips

xi.   2 scallions, thinly sliced

xii.   1 tbsp brown sugar

Method:

1. Combine vinegar, soy sauce, garlic, onions, brown sugar, pepper and bay leaf in the slow cooker. Add the chicken on top and sprinkle paprika.
2. Cover and cook for 8 hours on Low setting, or for 4 hours on High if preparing for lunch.
3. Turn the heat on High, if cooking on slow, in the last ten minutes.
4. Fold the bok choy in the chicken gently and cook for another 5 minutes.
5. Serve with rice and garnish with scallions.

19. Surf and Turf with Shrimp and Chicken

Serves: 8

Slow Cooker Size: 6- quart

Preparation time: 15 Minutes

Cooking Time: 5 Hours

Ingredients:

i. 4 skinless, boneless chicken thighs cut in small pieces

ii. 4 skinless, boneless chicken breasts, cut in small pieces

iii. 2 cups chopped onion

iv. 1 cup chopped celery

v. 1 cup chopped green pepper

vi. 2 garlic cloves, minced

vii. ½ tsp dried thyme

viii. 4 ounces turkey kielbasa (sausage), cut in thin slices

ix. 2 tsp Cajun seasoning

x. ¼ tsp Spanish smoked paprika

xi. 1 can fat-free chicken broth

xii.   1 pound medium shrimp, peeled and deveined

xiii.   1 tbsp hot sauce

xiv.   2 tbsp chopped parsley

xv.   2 ½ cups long-grain rice, cooked

xvi.   2 cans diced tomatoes with green peppers and onions, undrained

Method:

1. Heat a large skillet on high heat and cook the chicken on both sides until lightly browned, around 4 minutes. Add the chicken to the slow cooker

2. Add celery, bell pepper, onion and garlic in the skillet and cook until tender, around 4 minutes.

3. Add the turkey kielbasa, onion mixture, Cajun seasoning, dried thyme, tomatoes, paprika and chicken broth in the slow cooker.

4. Cover and cook on Low setting for 5 hours.

5. Add the cooked rice and the remaining ingredients in the slow cooker and cook on High setting for about 15 minutes, or until the shrimps are cooked.

20. Spicy Chicken Stew

Serves: 6

Slow Cooker Size: 5- quart

Preparation time: 10 Minutes

Cooking Time: 4 Hours

Ingredients:

i.   4 skinless, boneless chicken thighs

ii.   1 pound skinless, boneless chicken breast

iii.   2 baking potatoes, peeled and cut in cubes

iv.   2 celery stalks, chopped

v.   1 onion, roughly chopped

vi.   1 package frozen whole-kernel corn

vii.   2 carrots, peeled and cubed

viii. 2 ½ cups low-sodium chicken broth

ix.   2 garlic gloves, minced

x.   1 ½ tsp ground cumin

xi.   1 cup bottled salsa

xii.   1 tsp chili powder

xiii. Salt and pepper to taste

xiv.   4 corn tortillas, cut in strips

Method:

1. Add potatoes, corn, celery, carrots, onion and garlic in the slow cooker. Add salsa on top along with pepper, cumin and chili powder. Add the chicken on top of the vegetables. Pour the broth on top.
2. Cover and cook on High setting for 4 hours.
3. Remove the chicken and shred it using forks.
4. Place the rest of the vegetables and broth in a serving dish. Add shredded chicken and the tortilla strips in the stew.

21. Chicken Mole

Serves: 6

Slow Cooker Size: 5- 6- quart

Preparation time: 15 Minutes

Cooking Time: 4 Hours 15 Minutes

Ingredients:

i. 12 boneless, skinless chicken thighs

ii. 1 can whole tomatoes

iii. 2 dried ancho chiles, stemmed

iv. 1 medium onion, roughly chopped

v. 1 large chipotle chile in adobo sauce

vi. Salt to taste

vii. ¼ cup raisins

viii. ½ cup sliced almonds, toasted

ix. 3 garlic cloves, peeled and smashed

x. ¾ tsp ground cumin

xi. ½ cup bittersweet chocolate, finely chopped

xii. 3 tbsp extra-virgin olive oil

xiii. ½ tsp ground cinnamon

xiv. 2 cups boiled white rice

Method:

1. Season the chicken thighs with salt and place them in the slow cooker.
2. Puree the rest of the ingredients (except rice) in the blender. Add this mixture to the blender.
3. Cover and cook on Low setting for 8 hours or 4 hours on High if preparing for lunch.
4. Serve on top of a bed of rice.

22. Chicken with Garlic and Couscous

Serves: 4

Slow Cooker Size: 5- 6- quart

Preparation time: 25 Minutes

Cooking Time: 4 Hours

Ingredients:

i.   1 whole chicken, cut in 8 pieces

ii.   1 medium onion, thinly sliced

iii.   Salt and pepper to taste

iv.   1 tbsp extra-virgin olive oil

v.   1 cup dry white wine

vi.   6 garlic cloves, halved

vii.   1 cup couscous, cooked according to package instructions

viii. 1/3 cup all-purpose flour

ix.   2 tsp dried thyme

Method:

1. Season the chicken with salt and pepper and cook it on a large skillet until golden brown on all sides. Preferably cook in batches to ensure it is properly browned, should take about 4 minutes for each batch.

2. Add thyme, garlic and onion in the slow cooker. Add salt and pepper for seasoning. Layer the chicken on top of the onions in the slow cooker with skin side up. Be sure to make a tight layer.

3. Add wine and flour in a small bowl and whisk until blended. Add this to the slow cooker too.

4. Cover and cook on Low for 7 hours or for 3 ½ hours on High setting.

5. Serve the chicken over couscous.

23. Mexican Stew

Serves: 4

Slow Cooker Size: 5- quart

Preparation time: 20 Minutes

Cooking Time: 7 Hours

Ingredients:

- i.   4 skinless, boneless chicken breasts
- ii.   1 tbsp extra virgin olive oil
- iii. 1 medium onion, finely chopped
- iv.   ½ tsp dark brown sugar
- v.   1 (400g) can chopped tomatoes
- vi.   1 small red onion, sliced into rings
- vii. 1 tsp chipotle paste
- viii. 4 corn tortillas

Method:

1. Heat oil in a small skillet and sauté the onions. Add the onions along with the rest of the ingredients to the slow cooker.
2. Cover and cook on Low setting for 7 hours.

3. Remove the chicken and shred using two forks. Put the chicken back in the sauce.
4. Serve with tortillas.

24. Chicken Stew with White Wine

Serves: 4

Slow Cooker Size: 6- quart

Preparation time: 15 Minutes

Cooking Time: 4 Hours

Ingredients:

i.   1 pound skinless, boneless chicken breasts, cubed

ii.   1 cup chicken broth

iii.   3 tbsp olive oil

iv.   1 pound cremini mushrooms, quartered

v.   2 onions, sliced

vi.   2 Portobello mushrooms, sliced

vii.   1 cup dry white wine

viii. Salt and pepper to taste

Method:

1. Heat oil in a large skillet and cook the chicken until browned on both sides, around 5 minutes.
2. Add onions and mushroom in a saucepan and sate until both release their juices and turn golden brown. Be sure to continuously stir.
3. Add the onions and mushrooms to the slow cooker. Place chicken on top and season with salt and pepper.
4. Cover and cook on Low setting for 4 hours, or until the chicken is tender.

25. Chicken Stroganoff

Serves: 4

Slow Cooker Size: 5- quart

Preparation time: 15 Minutes

Cooking Time: 5 Hours 30 Minutes

Ingredients:

i. 4 skinless, boneless chicken breast halves, cubed

ii. 1 package cream cheese, 8 ounce

iii. 1 can condensed cream of chicken soup

iv. 1/8 cup margarine

v. 1 package dry Italian-style salad dressing mix

Method:

1. Add dressing mix, margarine and chicken in the slow cooker.
2. Cover and cook for 5 hours on Low setting.
3. Add the rest of the ingredients to the chicken and cook for another half hour on High setting.

26. BBQ Chicken

Serves: 4

Slow Cooker Size: 6- quart

Preparation time: 5 Minutes

Cooking Time: 4 Hours

Ingredients:

i.   3 large skinless chicken breasts, and bone-in
ii.   3 tbsp brown sugar
iii.   2 tbsp all purpose steak seasoning
iv.   1 cup BBQ sauce

Method:

1. Make 4 large balls from foil and fit them to the bottom of your slow cooker.
2. Season the chicken with brown sugar and steak seasoning
3. Place the chicken breasts on the foil balls in the slow cooker and pour the BBQ sauce over them.
4. Cover and cook on High setting for 4 hours or until the chicken is cooked.

5. Serve the chicken on a platter with remaining juices from the slow cooker poured over it.
6. You can also shred the chicken, mix it with the juices and serve with rice.

27. Lemon Chicken

Serves: 8

Slow Cooker Size: 5- 6- quart

Preparation time: 15 Minutes

Cooking Time: 6 Hours

Ingredients:

i.   12 boneless, skinless chicken thighs

ii.   1 cup low sodium chicken broth

iii. Salt and pepper to taste

iv.   1 lemon sliced,

v.   2 tbsp olive oil, divided

vi.   ¾ cup pitted green olives

vii. ¼ cup flour or cornstarch

viii. 2 tbsp lemon juice, freshly squeezed

Method:

1. Heat oil in a large skillet over medium heat and cook the chicken until browned on both sides, around six minutes. Preferably do it in batches.
2. Add the chicken to the slow cooker and cover with lemon slices.
3. Combine flour, cumin and juice and whisk until combined. Pour the broth over the chicken and top with olives and black pepper for seasoning.
4. Cover and cook for 6 hours on Low setting, or until well cooked.

28. Jamaican Chicken

Serves: 8

Slow Cooker Size: 6- quart

Preparation time: 15 Minutes

Cooking Time: 3 Hours

Ingredients:

i.   8 boneless skinless chicken breast halves
ii.   2 tbsp rice vinegar
iii.   2 tsp jerk seasoning
iv.   ½ cup light brown sugar
v.   1 ½ cups mango nectar
vi.   2 tbsp dark corn syrup

Method:

1. Add nectar, corn syrup, sugar, jerk seasoning and rice vinegar in the slow cooker and mix well. Add the chicken and coat it in the sauce.
2. Cover and cook on High setting for 3 hours.

29. Tea Smoked Chicken Legs

Serves: 6

Slow Cooker Size: 5- to 7- quart

Preparation time: 5 Minutes

Cooking Time: 5 Hours

Ingredients:

i.   6 skinless chicken legs

ii.   2 cups chicken broth

iii.   8 bags black tea

iv.   1 cinnamon stick

v.   4 slices ginger

vi.   ¼ cup hoisin sauce

vii.   ½ cup soy sauce

Method:

1. Boil the chicken broth in a saucepan and add the tea bags, cinnamon and ginger. Remove from heat and allow the broth to cool. Strain and mix hoisin and soy sauce.

2. Brush a little sauce on the legs. Pour the rest in the slow cooker. Add the chicken legs.

3. Cover and cook for 5 hours, basting the chicken 3 or 4 times during cooking.

30. Chicken Corn Soup

Serves: 6

Slow Cooker Size: 4- to 6- quart

Preparation time: 15 Minutes

Cooking Time: 8-9 Hours

Ingredients:

i. 1 pound boneless skinless chicken breast, cubed

ii. ½ tsp minced garlic

iii. 12 ounce cream style corn

iv. ½ cup chopped celery

v. ¾ cup sliced carrots

vi. 1 cup chopped onion

vii. Salt and pepper to taste

viii. 2 medium potatoes, cubed

ix. 12 ounces frozen corn

x. 2 cups low sodium chicken broth

Method:

1. Combine all the ingredients in the slow cooker.
2. Cover and cook for 8 hours.

Quick Slow Cooker Recipes

31. Chicken with Figs

Serves: 6

Slow Cooker Size: 5- 7- quart

Preparation time: 15 Minutes

Cooking Time: 2 Hours

Ingredients:

I.   6 boneless skinless chicken breast halves
II. 2 tbsp vegetable oil
III. Salt and freshly ground black pepper to taste
IV. ½ cup balsamic biegar
V.   ½ cup low-sodium chicken broth
VI. ½ cup Ruby Port
VII. 1 6 dried figs
VIII. 1 tsp dried thyme

Method:

1. Season the chicken with salt and pepper and cook it on a large skillet until both sides are golden brown, around 6 minutes.
2. Transfer the chicken to a slow cooker.
3. Scrape up the browns from the skillet using port and vinegar and pour it over the chicken.
4. Add the remaining ingredients.
5. Cover and cook on High setting for 2 hours.

32. Crockpot Pesto Chicken Thighs

Serves: 8

Slow Cooker Size: 6- quart

Preparation time: 15 Minutes

Cooking Time: 3 Hours

Ingredients:

i.   8 boneless chicken thighs

ii. 1 package seasoning mix

iii. ½ cup chicken broth

iv. 6 ounce jar of pesto

Method:

1. Place chicken thighs, ranch dressing, pesto and chicken broth in the slow cooker.
2. Cover and cook for two and a half hours on High setting, or until the chicken is cooked.

33. Sesame and Honey Wings

Serves: 4

Slow Cooker Size: 4- quart

Preparation time: 15 Minutes

Cooking Time: 2 Hours

Ingredients:

i.   1 1/2 pounds chicken wings

ii.   1/8 cup oil

iii. Salt and pepper to taste

iv.   1 cup honey

v.   ½ cup soy sauce

vi.   ¼ cup catsup

vii. 1 clove garlic, minced

viii. Sesame seeds for garnish

Method:

1. Place the wings in broiler pan and sprinkle salt and pepper on top. Place the pan about 5 inches under broiler and broil for 7 minutes on each side or until the chicken is golden.

2. Move the wings to the slow cooker and add the remaining ingredients, except the sesame seeds.

3. Cover and cook for 2 hours on High setting.

34. Tuscan Soup

Serves: 4

Slow Cooker Size: 5- quart

Preparation time: 15 Minutes

Cooking Time: 3 Hours

Ingredients:

i.   1 pound boneless, skinless chicken thighs, cut in small pieces

ii.   1 cup chopped onion

iii. Salt and freshly ground black pepper to taste

iv.   1 can low sodium chicken broth

v.   1 can cannellini beans, rinsed and drained

vi.   3 garlic cloves, minced

vii. 8 tbsp grated Parmesan cheese

viii. 1 package fresh baby spinach

ix.   ½ tsp chopped rosemary

x.   1 bottle roasted red bell peppers, drained and cut in small pieces

xi.   2 tbsp tomato paste

Method:

1. Add onions, tomato, beans, broth, bell peppers, salt and pepper, chicken and garlic in the slow cooker.
2. Cover and cook on High setting for an hour. Reduce the heat and then cook for another 2 hours, or until the chicken is fully cooked.
3. Add rosemary and spinach and cook for another 10 minutes on Low.
4. Serve the soup in bowls topped with cheese.

35. Chicken Cacciatore

Serves: 8

Slow Cooker Size: 5- quart

Preparation time: 15 Minutes

Cooking Time: 3 Hours

Ingredients:

i.   8 bone-in, skinned chicken drumsticks

ii.   8 bone-in, skinned chicken thighs

iii.   Salt and black pepper to taste

iv.   2 tbsp minced garlic

v.   1 tbsp olive oil

vi.   1 package mushrooms, quartered

vii.   1 large onion, sliced

viii.   1 red bell pepper, sliced

ix.   1 green bell pepper, sliced

x.   1/3 cup all purpose flour

xi.   2 tbsp chopped fresh thyme

xii.   2 tbsp chopped fresh oregano

xiii.   ½ cup red wine

xiv.   1 can whole plum tomatoes, chopped

Method:

1. Season the chicken with salt and pepper and cook on a skillet until lightly browned on both sides, around 6 minutes.
2. Add the chicken to the slow cooker and top it with the mushrooms.
3. Add bell peppers, garlic and onion to a pan and season with salt. Cook the vegetables for 5 minutes on medium heat. Add wine to the vegetables and cook for another minute, scraping the brown bits off. Add oregano, tomatoes, flour and thyme.
4. Add this tomato mixture to the chicken in the slow cooker.
5. Cover and cook for 3 hours on High setting.
6. Preferably serve with fettuccine.

36.Chicken Ginger and Sesame Lunch Special

Serves: 4

Slow Cooker Size: 4- quart

Preparation time: 15 Minutes

Cooking Time: 2 ½ Hours

Ingredients:

i.   8 bone-in chicken thighs, skinned

ii.   ¼ cup soy sauce

iii.   5 tsp hoisin sauce

iv.   1 tbsp sesame oil

v.   2 tbsp light brown sugar

vi.   1 tbsp cornstarch

vii.   2 tbsp fresh orange juice

viii.   2 tsp sesame seeds, toasted

ix.   1 tbsp cold water

x.   2 tbsp sliced green onions

xi.   1 tbsp minced ginger

xii.   1 tsp minced garlic

Method:

1. Cook the chicken in batches in a large skillet until golden brown, ideally 5 minutes.
2. Transfer chicken to the slow cooker.
3. Add soy sauce, garlic, brown sugar, hoisin sauce, ginger and orange juice in a medium sized bowl and pour over the chicken.
4. Cover and cook on Low setting for 2 ½ hours or until the chicken is tender. Transfer chicken to the serving platter.
5. Sieve the sauce in the slow cooker and bring it to a boil in over medium heat. Discard the solids. S
6. Combine cornstarch and cold water and pour it in the sauce to make it thick. Cook for another minute and pour the sauce over the chicken.
7. Sprinkle green onions and sesame seed on top.

37. Spinach Stuffed Chicken Breasts

Serves: 6

Slow Cooker Size: 6- 7- quart

Preparation time: 15 Minutes

Cooking Time: 3 Hours

Ingredients:

i. 6 boneless skinless breast halves

ii. 2 tbsp olive oil

iii. Salt and pepper to taste

iv. One packet of frozen chopped spinach, defrosted and squeezed dry

v. 1 ½ cups chicken broth

vi. ¼ tsp freshly grated nutmet

vii. ¼ cup finely chopped shallot

viii. ½ cup dry white wine

ix. 1 cup heavy cream

x. ¼ cup finely chopped chives

xi. One package Boursin cheese, 2-ounce

Method:

1. Place the chicken in plastic wraps and pound until the chicken gets a uniform thickness. Season it with salt and pepper.

2. Sauté the shallots in oil in a medium sized skillet, for about 2 minutes. Add spinach and cook until wilted. Season with salt, pepper and nutmeg and stir well. Once cool at Boursin cheese.

3. Spread the shallot stuffing on the chicken breasts. Roll up the chicken breasts and tuck sides to enclose the filling.

4. Now lay these seam side down in the slow cooker and pour the wine on top. Use skewers if the rolls aren't properly secured.

5. Cover and cook on high setting for 2 ½ hours.

6. Carefully remove the chicken and cover with foil. Pour the sauce in a saucepan and bring to a boil. Cook for another five minutes or until the sauce is reduced to half. Bring the heat to low and add the cream. Remove from heat and stir in chives.

7. Cu each chicken breast into 4 pieces crosswise.

8. Serve the chicken with the sauce.

Special Recipes for Special Occasions

38. Chicken and Red Wine Casserole

Serves: 6

Slow Cooker Size: 4- quart

Preparation time: 15 Minutes

Cooking Time: 8 Hours

Ingredients:

i. 6 bone-in chicken breasts
ii. 3 tbsp olive oil
iii. 3 tbsp plain flour
iv. 3 onions, cut in wedges
v. 3 garlic cloves
vi. 200g smoked bacon lardons
vii. 300g flat mushrooms, sliced
viii. 2 tbsp redcurrant sauce
ix. 1 cup red wine

x.   3 strips of orange zest

xi.   1 cup low-sodium chicken stock

xii.   2 bay leaves

Method:

1. Season the chicken with salt and pepper and cook on medium heat in a large skillet until lightly browned on both sides, around five minutes.

2. Add the onions and lardons and cook for another 6 minutes. Sprinkle the plain flour and add garlic and cook for another minute. Be sure to keep on stirring to avoid sticking.

3. Add the chicken and bacon along with the remaining ingredients in the slow cooker and cook on Low heat for 8 hours.

39. Orange Cranberry Chicken

Serves: 6

Slow Cooker Size: 5- quart

Preparation time: 15 Minutes

Cooking Time: 6 Hours

Ingredients:

i. 6 skinless, boneless chicken breast halves, cut in small pieces
ii. 1 cup low-sodium chicken broth
iii. 1 tbsp margarine
iv. ¼ cup brown sugar
v. 1 tsp chopped ginger
vi. 1/3 cup reduced-sugar orange marmalade
vii. 1 tbsp rice vinegar
viii. ½ tsp ground cinnamon
ix. ½ cup dried cranberries

Method:

1. Add all the ingredients, except chicken, in the slow cooker and blend well.
2. Place the chicken on the top, cover and cook on Low setting for 6 hours.
3. Serve with the sauce, preferably with brown rice.

40. Chicken Pesto Potato

Serves: 4

Slow Cooker Size: 5- quart

Preparation time: 15 Minutes

Cooking Time: 6 Hours

Ingredients:

i.   4 skinless, boneless chicken breasts

ii.   4 tbsp prepared pesto

iii.   1 ½ tsp olive oil

iv.   1 tsp lemon pepper seasoning

v.   ½ cup low-sodium chicken broth

vi.   4 cups potato pieces, partially cooked in the microwave

vii.   ½ cup chopped red bell pepper

Method:

1. Heat a large nonstick pan and cook the chicken breasts with olive oil until lightly browned on both sides, around 6 minutes.
2. Add the potato pieces to the slow cooker and pour the chicken broth on top.

3. Spread pesto evenly over the top and sprinkle with red pepper. Gently toss the mixture and place the chicken on top.
4. Cover and cook for about 6 hours on Low setting.

41. Chicken Vegetable Soup with Noodles

Serves: 6

Slow Cooker Size: 4- to 6- quart

Preparation time: 15 Minutes

Cooking Time: 7 Hours

Ingredients:

i. 3 pound chicken

ii. 2 cups sliced carrots

iii. 2 cups chopped onion

iv. 1 cup uncooked egg noodles

v. 2 cups celery

vi. Salt and pepper to taste

vii. ½ tsp basil

viii. 10 ounces frozen peas

ix. 2 tbsp parsley

x. 2 cups water

xi. ¼ tsp thyme

Method:

1. Add all the ingredients in the slow cooker except noodles, place chicken on top of the rest of the ingredients.
2. Cover and cook for 6 hours on Low setting.
3. Add the noodles, cover and cook on High setting for another hour.

42. Peanut Butter Wings

Serves: 8

Slow Cooker Size: 6- quart

Preparation time: 20 Minutes

Cooking Time: 3-4 Hours

Ingredients:

i.   3 pounds chicken wings

ii.   Salt and pepper to taste

iii.   ¼ cup olive oil

iv.   1 tsp paprika

v.   ½ cup chicken broth

vi.   2 tbsp soy sauce

vii.   ¼ tsp hot sauce

viii.   2 tsp grated ginger

ix.   ¼ cup brown sugar

x.   1 cup smooth peanut butter

xi.   1 can coconut milk, 14-ounce

xii.   ½ cup roasted peanuts, finely chopped

Method:

1. Put the wings, olive oil, paprika, pepper and salt in a large bowl and mix well until the wings are well coated. Arrange the wings on a baking sheet and broil in a preheated broiler for about 5 minutes on each side, or until crispy brown.
2. Combine all the remaining ingredients, except peanuts, in a saucepan over medium heat and cook for 2 minutes. Pour the sauce over the wings.
3. Transfer the sauce and the wings in the slow cooker.
4. Cover and cook for 3 hours.
5. Serve with a garnish of peanuts.

Slow Cooker Recipes Your Kids Will Love

43. Chili Chicken Tacos

Serves: 4

Slow Cooker Size: 4- quart

Preparation time: 15 Minutes

Cooking Time: 4 Hours

Ingredients:

i. 6 boneless, skinless chicken thighs

ii. ½ cup prepared tomato salsa

iii. 4 garlic cloves

iv. 1 tbsp chili powder

v. 2 tbsp chopped canned chipotle chiles in adobo

vi. Salt and pepper to taste

vii. 8 hard corn taco shells

viii. 1 tbsp chili powder

Method:

1. Combine chicken, salsa, garlic, chili powder, chiles and salt and pepper.
2. Cover and cook on Low setting for 8 hours.
3. Transfer the chicken in a bowl and shred using two forks. Place it back in the slow cooker juices and serve in taco shells.
4. You can also top the shells with shredded cheese, sour cream or lime wedges, depending on your children's preferences.

44. Juicy Chicken Burgers

Serves: 8

Slow Cooker Size: 5- quart

Preparation time: 25 Minutes

Cooking Time: 4 Hours

Ingredients:

i.   1 pound boneless, skinless chicken thighs cut in small pieces

ii. 1 pound boneless, skinless chicken breasts cut in small pieces

iii. 1 tbsp extra virgin olive oil

iv. Salt and pepper to taste

v.   1 medium onion, diced

vi. 1 medium red bell pepper, seeded and diced

vii. 3 cloves garlic, roughly chopped

viii. 1 can crushed tomatoes

ix. 3 tbsp Worcestershire sauce

x.   ¼ cup hot-pepper sauce

xi. 2 tbsp yellow mustard

xii. 1 tbsp molasses

xiii. 8 buns

Method:

1. Season the chicken with salt and pepper and cook on a large skillet in oil until golden brown on both sides, will take around 6 minutes.
2. Place the chicken in the slow cooker.
3. Add onions, bell pepper and garlic in the skillet and cook over medium heat for about 6 minutes or until the onions become translucent. Add ¼ cup of water and cook for another five minutes. Scrape the brown bits off from sides and season with salt and pepper.
4. Add this mixture to the slow cooker and top with the rest of the ingredients, except the buns.
5. Cover and cook on High setting for 4 hours.
6. Take out the chicken, shred using forks and mix it with the sauce again.
7. Serve on buns.

45. Cheesy Chicken and Broccoli

Serves: 4

Slow Cooker Size: 5- quart

Preparation time: 10 Minutes

Cooking Time: 7 Hours 20 Minutes

Ingredients:

i.   4 boneless, skinless chicken breasts

ii. 1 ½ cup chicken broth

iii. 1 can cream of cheddar soup

iv. 1 can cream of chicken soup

v.   ¾ cup sour cream

vi. 3 tsp garlic powder

vii. 6 cups broccoli florets, cooked

viii. 2 cup cooked rice

Method:

1. Add chicken broth, cream of cheddar, cream of chicken, garlic powder and salt to the slow cooker and mix well. Add the chicken on the top.
2. Cover and cook on Low setting for 7 hours.
3. Transfer the chicken in a large bowl and shred using two forks.
4. Add the cooked broccoli and sour cream and cook for another 20 minutes on Low setting.
5. Serve with rice.

46. Juicy Chicken Breasts

Serves: 4

Slow Cooker Size: 5- quart

Preparation time: 15 Minutes

Cooking Time: 4 Hours

Ingredients:

i.   4 bone-in, skin on chicken breasts

ii. 2 tsp paprika

iii. 2 tbsp all purpose steak seasoning

Method:

1. Lay the bottom of the slow cooker with 5 foil balls.
2. Season the chicken breasts with paprika and steak seasoning.
3. Lay the chicken breasts on top of the foil in the slow cooker and cook on High setting for 4 hours.
4. Transfer the chicken on the serving dish and brush it with the juices from the slow cooker.

47. Chicken Teriyaki

Serves: 4

Slow Cooker Size: 5- quart

Preparation time: 15 Minutes

Cooking Time: 7 Hours

Ingredients:

i.   6 boneless chicken thighs

ii. 2 tbsp grated ginger

iii. 2 tbsp brown sugar

iv. ½ cup low sodium soy sauce

v.   2 garlic cloves, minced

Method:

1. Add the chicken in the slow cooker along with the rest of the ingredients.
2. Cover and cook on High for one hour and then reduce the heat and cook on Low setting for 6 hours.
3. Serve on a bed of cooked rice or shred it and make sandwiches.

48. Chicken Meat Balls

Serves: 6

Slow Cooker Size: 6- 7- quart

Preparation time: 25 Minutes

Cooking Time: 7-8 Hours

Ingredients:

For Marinara

I.   2 tbsp extra virgin olive oil

II. Pinch red pepper flakes

III. 1 medium onion, finely chopped

IV. 1 tsp dried basil

V.   Two cans crushed tomatoes

VI. Salt and pepper to taste

VII. ½ cup finely chopped Italian parsley

For Chicken Meatballs

I.   2 pounds chicken

II. ¼ cup milk

III. 1 large egg, beaten

IV. 1 cup bread crumbs

V.   2 tbsp Italian parsley

VI.   ½ cup grated Parmesan cheese

VII.   ½ cup finely chopped onion

VIII.   Salt to taste

IX.   1 clove garlic, minced

Method:

1. Heat oil in a small pan and sauté onion, garlic, basil and pepper flakes, around 5 minutes.
2. Transfer the onion mixture to the slow cooker and add salt, pepper, tomatoes and parsley on top. Mix well.
3. Cover and cook for 3 hours on Low setting.
4. Meanwhile, add the bread crumbs and milk in a large mixing bowl and mix. Add the rest of the ingredients and blend well.
5. Form 2-inch balls from the mixture. Transfer the meatballs in the slow cooker and gently spoon some of the sauce over them.
6. Cover and cook for an additional 3 hours, or until the meatballs are fully cooked.

49. Smokey Chicken

Serves: 5

Slow Cooker Size: 4- quart

Preparation time: 15 Minutes

Cooking Time: 7 Hours

Ingredients:

i.   3 pounds skinned chicken pieces, including breast halves and thighs

ii.   Salt and pepper to taste

iii.   1 cup chicken broth

iv.   ½ cup snipped dried apricots

v.   1 tbsp quick cooking tapioca, finely ground

vi.   1 tbsp adobo sauce

vii.   2 canned chipotle chile peppers in adobo sauce, chopped

viii.   111/2 cup raspberry jam

Method:

1. Season the chicken pieces with salt and pepper and place them in the slow cooker.
2. Stir raspberry jam, chipotle sauce, broth, adobo sauce and tapioca in a small bowl and pour over the chicken pieces.
3. Cover and cook on Low setting for 7 hours.

50. Puttanesca Chicken

Serves: 6

Slow Cooker Size: 4- quart

Preparation time: 20 Minutes

Cooking Time: 7 Hours

Ingredients:

i.   3 pounds skinless chicken pieces including drumsticks, thighs and breast halves

ii.   26 ounce jar pasta sauce with olives

iii.   Salt and pepper to taste

iv.   3 cups cooked orzo pasta

v.   2 tsp finely shredded lemon peel

vi.   2 tbsp drained capers

Method:

1. Season the chicken pieces with salt and pepper and place them in the slow cooker.
2. Mix capers, lemon peel and pasta sauce in a bowl and pour it over the chicken pieces.
3. Cover and cook on Low setting for 7 hours.
4. Serve the chicken over cooked orzo.

CONCLUSION

There you go! Scrumptiously divine chicken slow-cooker recipes to make each day, night, and special occasion feast a memorable one. Now you can easily throw away your Crock-pot carton, because from now on, your slow cooker will not need to be boxed ever again!

The greatest thing about slow cooker recipes are that they fit in well with a fast paced lives making it the perfect solution for working individuals and parents to easily prepare delectable meals. Simply prepare the ingredients in less than 15 minutes in the morning and come home to steaming hot and deliciously desirable meals in the evening.

Time to get inventive and start cooking!

15883446R00064

Printed in Great Britain
by Amazon